MORAL DILEMMAS

CENSORSHIP

Philip Steele

Evans

EVANS BROTHERS LIMITED

First published in 1999 by
Evans Brothers Limited

Evans Brothers Limited
2a Portman Mansions
Chiltern Street
London W1M 1LE

© Evans Brothers Limited 1999

Editor: Su Swallow
Design: Neil Sayer and Tinstar Design
Production: Jenny Mulvanny
Picture research: Victoria Brooker

Printed in Hong Kong by Wing King Tong Co. Ltd.

British Library Cataloguing in Publication Data

Steele, Philip
  Censorship. - (Moral dilemmas)
  1. Censorship - Juvenile literature
  2. Censorship - History - Juvenile literature
  I. Title
  363.3'1

  ISBN 0237518783

ACKNOWLEDGEMENTS

For permission to reproduce copyright material, the author
and publishers gratefully acknowledge the following:

Cover (central image) Abass/Magnum (back
cover) Rex Features
page 6 E.T. Archive **page 8** Link Picture Library
page 9 Tim Page/Corbis **page 10** Nina
Berman/Rex Features **page 12** B. Moser/The
Hutchison Library **page 13** Kevin Fleming/
Corbis **page 15** Alex Webb/Magnum **page 16**
Jennie Woodcock; Reflections Photolibrary/
Corbis **page 18** Corbis-Bettman/UPI **page 19**
Rex Features **page 20** Abass/Magnum **page 22**
Greg English/Link Picture Library **page 23** The
National Archives/Corbis **page 24** Prado,
Madrid/Index/The Bridgeman Art Library **page
28** Anne Griffiths Belt/Corbis **page 30** Alex
Webb/Magnum **page 31** J. Horner/SOA
Hutchison Library **page 32** Associated
Press/Topham **page 33** Hulton-Deutsch
Collection/Corbis **page 34** Peter
Marlow/Magnum Photos **page 37** Tsafrir
Abayov/Link Picture Library **page 38** Jennie
Woodcock; Reflections Photolibrary/Corbis
page 40 Musee Carnavalet, Paris/Bulloz/The
Bridgeman Art Library **page 41** Ian McIlgorm/
Rex Features **page 44** David Beatty/Robert
Harding Picture Library **page 45** *Combat of
Gladiators in the Arena* 1948 by Giorgio de
Chirico, © DACS London 1998/Galleria
Nationale d'Arte Moderne, Rome/Peter
Willi/The Bridgeman Art Library **page 47** H.P.
Merten/ Robert Harding Picture Library **page
48** Rex Features **page 50** R. Trippett/Rex
Features **page 51** Topham Picture Point **page 52**
Rex Features **page 55** Antonio Alonso/
Associated Press **page 56** Harry Cabluck/
Associated Press **page 58** Susan Walsh/
Associated Press

CONTENTS

1. WHAT IS CENSORSHIP?

You may not have heard of the first emperor of China, Qin Shi Huangdi. However, you may well have seen pictures of his famous tomb. It was surrounded by a fantastic army, made up of thousands of life-sized model soldiers buried in the ground. This man was so desperate for power that he still wanted to issue commands from the grave. He was a cruel ruler, who couldn't stand any criticism or opposition. Around the year 213BC, Qin Shi Huangdi became afraid that historians might write bad things about his reign. He ordered all books that weren't about strictly practical subjects to be collected up and publicly burned. It is said that when various scholars and officials disagreed with him, he had 460 of them buried alive.

This may be ancient history – but similar events are taking place in many parts of the world even as you read this book. Videos, plays, films or television programmes are banned. Laws are passed to limit use of the internet. Critics of powerful politicians are imprisoned, tortured or even murdered if they speak their mind. It is called censorship.

Books were burned and opposing voices were silenced by the first emperor of all China, Qin Shi Huangdi. He used strict censorship to control the country and to protect his reputation.

> **Every society has a right to preserve public peace and order, and therefore has a good right to prohibit the propagation of opinions which have a dangerous tendency.**
>
> *Samuel Johnson,*
> *English writer (1709-84)*

Censorship is any attempt to limit or prevent the free exchange of information. Of course all communication is limited or selected to some degree. We censor ourselves every time we decide what to put in a letter and what to leave out. However, if someone else refuses us permission to send a letter, or says we can only write about certain subjects, that is a clear case of censorship.

Censorship can work in other ways, too. It can be a refusal to communicate at all. For example, a big company may refuse to disclose facts that the public should know about its products. Such secrecy can be used to prevent the fair exchange of information, as can putting out false information or presenting it in a dishonest or confusing way.

Where did the idea of censorship first come from? It is certainly older than that Chinese emperor, and is probably as old as human society itself. From the year 443BC the ancient Romans employed public officials called 'censors'. Their job was not only to count the number of Roman citizens (in a 'census'), but also to check up on whether people were suitable to be citizens in the first place. Were they loyal? Were they moral? If a poet published verse that made fun of the government, the censors could send him into exile. Later, some emperors appointed themselves as official censors. They realised the political power that this gave them.

Censorship isn't always carried out by power-crazed rulers or governments. It is often used to benefit or protect people. For example, most parents would wish to prevent their children from seeing violent videos or obscene magazines, or from accessing offensive material on the internet. In a similar way many governments pass laws in order to protect their citizens from abuse, from persecution or offence, however caused. Censorship, like other forms of social control, can be used for good or for evil.

> **There should be no censorship of any kind.**
>
> *Camille Paglia, US writer and*
> *lecturer, 1994*

2. COMMUNICATION AND THE MEDIA

Humans need to communicate in order to survive. From the moment babies are born, they cry to let their parents know when they are hungry or tired. Growing children soon have to master a whole range of words, expressions and gestures to help them interact with the rest of society. Humans have developed communication to a more advanced state than any other creatures on Earth.

> **...the Word, written or spoken, is our precious common property.**
>
> *Nadine Gordimer,*
> *South African writer, 1997*

Individuals or small groups of people may communicate by word of mouth, by post, by phone, e-mail or fax. People with speech and hearing problems may communicate by signing with their hands.

To reach a larger number of people, it may be necessary to call a public meeting or hold a lecture. To spread the message further still, we may publish books, newspapers, magazines, photographs or advertisements. We may broadcast by radio or television, on film or video. We may put a message across through the arts, exhibiting paintings or sculpture, putting on plays, or recording music. We may use the internet to exchange information electronically, computer-to-computer worldwide.

At Speakers' Corner, in Hyde Park, anyone has the right to stand up and speak. Members of the public often heckle, shouting out their disagreement with the speaker. This is free speech in action, but the audience is limited and the influence of the speaker may be small.

Q

Does the nature of the medium we use affect the type of message we send?

Media power

These methods of presentation are all known as communications 'media'. A medium is any channel for exchanging information. Communications media clearly have the power to influence people and shape public opinion. Indeed, that is one of their main aims. That is why politicians worry about election broadcasts, why companies pay huge sums to advertise in the media, why the first aim of revolutionaries is to capture the government radio station.

Media coverage of the Vietnam War often showed the grim reality of jungle warfare. Coverage of later conflicts was more closely controlled.

Bringing the war back home

During the 1960s and 1970s, the United States of America fought a long and bitter war in Vietnam, in Southeast Asia. It was the first war of the television age. Night after night, pictures of violence and bloodshed were shown on television news back home in the USA. It is widely believed that these images helped to turn American public opinion against the war. During more recent conflicts, such as the Gulf War of 1990-91, the images shown by US, British and other European media were strictly limited. Images of suffering were rarely shown on television news, and anti-war protests back at home were largely ignored. The censors had realised the power of television as a medium.

Q *Governments often control the media. Is it possible for the media to control governments?*

The power of the media can extend far into the future. The version of events described in a book or film may be the only one that goes down in history, to be remembered by future generations. The winners of wars and political struggles may rewrite history. By controlling our understanding of the past, they can influence the present.

The more people that a medium reaches, the more powerful it can be. Originally, news was a local affair, passed from village to village by word of mouth. Today satellites in space can beam news reports around the world in a flash. In the USA, a single television broadcast of the 1996 Superbowl reached over 138 million viewers. In 1997 a Japanese newspaper called *Yomiuri Shimbun* was selling over 14 million copies a day.

The media empire of businessman Rupert Murdoch gives him great power. When he speaks about media and government controls, that in itself makes news.

Should governments place limits on the amount of media that may be owned by one person?

Access to the media

If control of the media brings power and influence, then access to the media makes people a part of the same equation. Although worldwide audiences may be huge, there are areas which the media barely reach. In many parts of Africa, for example, there are relatively few newspapers, a limited number of televisions and very few personal computers. Most ordinary people simply cannot afford to buy them. The public is excluded and this makes it harder for them to be informed about issues that affect them and harder too for them to get a hearing. Their voice is ignored and that makes them less influential in the world.

In many countries only a small number of wealthy or influential people – an elite – can afford access to media such as the internet. The media returns the favour by reporting mostly the views and activities of rich and powerful people. Does this give the elite an unfair advantage over poorer sections of society?

Free speech – at a price?
Which countries are rich enough to plug into the communications media? These charts show those countries with most media access. Not one African country appears. The world's biggest country, the Russian Federation, doesn't appear. China, the world's most populous country, appears only under book sales. The other Asian giant, India, is completely absent. Media access is largely the privilege of the world's richest countries.

Television ownership (Number of people per set)	Video-cassette recorder owners (Percentage of households owning)
1 Bermuda 0.9	1 United Kingdom 86%
2 United States 1.3	2 United States 79%
3 Australia 1.6	3 Japan 76%
Brunei 1.6	4 Belgium 73%
Canada 1.6	5 Italy 72%
Japan 1.6	6 Denmark 71%
United Kingdom 1.6	Luxembourg 71%
8 France 1.7	8 Canada 69%
Luxembourg 1.7	Finland 69%
10 Germany 1.8	Sweden 69%
Norway 1.8	

Book sales(US$m)	Internet sites
1 United States 25,490	1 United States 10,267,901
2 Japan 10,467	2 United Kingdom 733,538
3 Germany 9,962	3 Japan 732,898
4 United Kingdom 3,651	4 Germany 721,291
5 France 3,380	5 Canada 599,213
6 Spain 2,992	6 Australia 509,360
7 S Korea 2,805	7 Finland 283,490
8 Brazil 2,526	8 Netherlands 270,395
9 Italy 2,246	9 France 245,199
10 China 1,760	10 Sweden 231,915

Source: *The Economist: Pocket World in Figures*, 1998 ed

Young children gather around a television set in Guyaquil, in the South American country of Ecuador. The programme they are watching probably bears little relation to their everyday life. Many programmes made in the richer parts of the world are exported to poorer countries.

Q *Might it be said that poverty and illiteracy – being unable to read and write – is a form of censorship imposed on the poor by the rich?*

New technologies

All channels of communication, from the simplest to the most complex, may be targeted by the censors. However, as soon as one medium has been brought under control, a new medium springs up to take its place. It is as if the censors are trying to dam a brook with mud and sticks. The water keeps finding a new route around the edge.

During the Middle Ages in Europe, about 600 years ago, books were handwritten and their content was mostly controlled by the Roman Catholic Church or by the royal courts. Along came the new technology of printing, and suddenly anyone could publish their ideas.

Almost immediately offices of religious censorship were set up to produce lists of prohibited books, and soon printers were having to be licensed by the government.

In the first half of the twentieth century, new media arrivals included radio and television. For the first time ever, information could be beamed over national frontiers.

Even when two countries were hostile, or following very different political systems, their citizens could tune in to communications from the other side. Governments sometimes responded by blocking broadcasts from other lands with interference, a technique called 'jamming'.

In the 1990s new technology made the internet possible – and immediately laws were introduced in Europe, Australia and North America to bring the new medium to heel. In 1996, the state government of Western Australia passed new censorship laws to meet the age of new technology. It announced that in future it would censor all offensive material from computer transmissions, such as e-mail, internet, online computer services and local networks. In 1997, Germany brought in new laws which required internet service providers to be officially licensed, just as printers had been 400 years before them.

A cup of coffee and a chance to 'surf' attracts customers to an internet café. Exploring information sources worldwide is fun – but it has its dangers. Should it be controlled?

The media's message

We tend to think that the media are neutral carriers of information, that 'if it's in the newspapers, it must be true'. The first question we should ask is: what do we mean by 'true'? Two reporters assigned to cover the same story may produce two very different versions of events. They may have different personal views which colour their writing. A questioning approach is particularly important when using the internet. There is no guarantee that the information provided at a website is accurate or unbiased.

> **When news breaks, we fix it.**
>
> *The Daily Show,
> Comedy Channel, USA*

The second question we should ask is: which forces are affecting the medium in question? For example, who owns and controls it? Does it have a purpose other than the straightforward communication of information? Does it make money by advertising as well as sales? Is it operating under any laws which limit what it can say? Is it liable to be shut down if it offends the authorities?

> *How can we have a mature democracy when newspapers and television are beginning to be so interlaced in ownership? Where are our freedoms to be guaranteed? Who is going to guarantee them?*
>
> *Dennis Potter, English playwright, 1994*

Commercial interests

In 1998 the HarperCollins company scrapped plans to publish the memoirs of Chris Patten, the last governor of Hong Kong. This British colony had passed back to Chinese rule in 1997, and in his book Patten had written a stinging condemnation of the Chinese government. Rupert Murdoch, head of News Corporation and owner of HarperCollins, had important business interests in China. Critics claimed that this was the reason for stopping publication and that the medium should have remained neutral. Others claimed that as the publisher, Murdoch had every right not to print a title with which he disagreed, and that providing a neutral medium should form no part of a publishers' duties. They said that because Patten could always publish the book elsewhere, it was not a suppression of free expression.

> **He who pays the piper calls the tune.**
> *English proverb*

> **The truth is partisan.**
> *Vladimir Ilyich Lenin,
> Russian revolutionary
> (1870-1924)*

The publicising of a particular viewpoint or political line is called propaganda. We have to learn to separate fact from opinion by studying each article or programme very closely. The lines between the two are not always clear-cut. A reporter's personal impression can often tell us far more than a recital of the bare facts. But at least we should compare different reports to get a broader picture before we form our own judgement.

Of course, all communication may include personal opinions. There is nothing wrong with that. Indeed, they are part of the joy of communicating. We just have to make sure that we don't accept everything we see, hear and read too readily. All the media are subject to censorship. Members of the public must remember to treat everything they read or watch with a large pinch of salt.

Q *Can any medium be completely independent? Don't all media owners have their own agenda, even if it's only to make money?*

A free press serves a vital role in bringing us news of conflicts from around the world. During the 1990s, reporters filed stories about troubled politics on the Caribbean island of Haiti.

3. WHO INTERFERES – AND WHY?

Censorship may start in the classroom. In 1997, an English girl called Sarah Briggs was expelled from her school in Mansfield for criticising her teachers in the local newspaper. In the same year an Australian education minister approved the removal of a play called *Top Girls* by Caryl Churchill from a Higher School Certificate reading list in New South Wales, claiming that the play was dated, violent and irreligious.

You, too, have probably experienced some sort of censorship in your everyday life. For example,

Learning science. Some parents may reject scientific theories which disagree with their religious beliefs. Should these parents be allowed to withold their children from class?

laws or other rules lay down which subjects you may or may not be taught in class. Your parents may refuse you permission to watch a film on television or to attend a concert at some club. You may be barred from buying a ticket at the cinema because you are too young to see the film being shown.

> *Corporate giants can regularly distort and censor news presentation to serve their requirements.*
>
> Philip Jones Griffiths, former head of Magnum Photos, 1997

Q *Who should control what you are taught in school – the government, the local council, teachers, parents or pupils?*

People in power

Who are behind acts of censorship? Which groups of people pull the strings of the media? To start with, there are those who have political power, and those who make or enforce the law. Examples might include rulers, democratic presidents as well as unelected dictators, national or regional governments and councils, political parties, armies, judges, police forces and customs officers. Then there are those who have industrial power, such as big companies and corporations, professional bodies and advertisers, and trade unions.

There are churches and religious leaders of all faiths. There are people who are responsible for bringing up children, such as parents and teachers. Then there are the 'middle-men and -women' – the people who operate the media, delivering or distributing the message to the public, such as publishers, editors, booksellers, librarians, newsagents, cinema owners, television presenters. And finally there is you, a member of the public. You too are a censor in that you can switch off a programme, refuse to buy goods or start up pressure groups for media campaigns or boycotts.

So censorship can be carried out by almost anyone in society who has the power, organisation or ability to do so. In fact there has never been a society in the world in which censorship has not existed in one form or another. The only difference has been in the degree. Dictatorships rely heavily on censorship to control the people, while democracies normally use censorship to prevent the abuse of power.

Political censorship

What kind of material is commonly censored? Political ideas have always been one of the most sensitive areas. Governments are often afraid of anyone who challenges the existing system.

During the early 1950s, a 'Cold War' divided the world's most powerful countries, because they followed different political systems. Russia, which was then part of the Soviet Union, was feared by the western countries as communist. Its economy was mostly controlled by the state and the only real political power lay with the Communist Party. Anyone who criticised the Party and its ideas could find themselves sentenced to long years of hard labour in a remote prison camp.

The United States, on the other hand, was capitalist, with both of its main parties supporting the interests of big business. It prided itself on being a democracy, and yet a US senator called Joseph ('Joe') McCarthy was able to start up a virulent campaign against people he accused of being communists, especially those working in the media. Many of them were not communists at all, but they were still blacklisted, sacked, refused new employment and publicly harassed.

In 1953 leading US citizens, including many media-workers, were interrogated by Senator McCarthy's Subcommittee on Investigations. They were accused, often falsely, of being communists. This was a form of censorship by public intimidation.

No truth please – it hurts!
Political censorship is still common all around the world today. In 1997 the Croatian government, in southern Europe, brought in laws under which journalists could be prosecuted for writing 'insulting' reports – even if their facts were proved to be correct!

Moral judgements

All sorts of magazines, films, videos, computer games, internet sites and other media may be outlawed for moral reasons. Some are condemned as obscene, which means that they offend against society's idea of what is decent. Obscene material which is intended to be sexually stimulating is called pornography.

The notion of what is immoral and what isn't may vary greatly from one culture to another and from one generation to the next. For example, in many Islamic countries, such as Pakistan, kissing scenes may be cut from films as immoral.

Q A modern photograph of a nude body may be called obscene, while a medieval painting of the same subject may be called a masterpiece. Is this hypocritical? Does the nature of the media or its age affect our judgement of its content?

A huge range of publications go on sale around the world every day. Some may cause offence to many members of the public. Should their display or sale be restricted? Should they be banned completely?

Other films and publications are condemned for being too violent. The term 'gratuitous' is often used to describe violence which seems to serve no purpose other than entertainment.

Muslim demonstrators around the world showed their opposition to the author Salman Rushdie, accused of blasphemy against Islam (see page 21). Should books be banned if they offend people's religious beliefs, or should writers be free to express their views?

Faith and beliefs

Another sensitive area surrounds deeply-held religious beliefs. Insulting somebody's faith in God is called blasphemy. Putting forward an idea that is not approved by one's religious leaders is called heresy. In some countries these are considered to be deadly sins and may be punished by death. Those people leading religious censorship campaigns are often referred to as fundamentalists, people who believe that their holy scriptures are the only ones to be true in every detail.

> **He who forsakes the Law of Islam should be fought.**
>
> *Ibn Taymiyya, Egyptian Islamic scholar (1263-1328)*

> **It is a public crime to act as though there is no God.**
>
> *Pope Leo XIII, 1885*

The force of the fatwa

When a British writer called Salman Rushdie published a novel called The Satanic Verses *in 1988, many Muslims declared it to be blasphemous. The leader of Iran at that time, Ayatollah Khomeini, pronounced a* fatwa *or prohibition order against the author, calling on Muslims all over the world to kill him. Salman Rushdie was forced into hiding for many years. The man who translated the book into Japanese, Hitoshi Igarishi, was murdered in 1991. Ten years after publication, Rushdie remained unforgiven by the Iranian authorities.*

In most other countries the laws regarding religious matters are less harsh, whilst in some religion is regarded as no concern of the state or the legal system, but a matter for the individual. Some twentieth-century governments, from Albania to China, at times actively censored religious expression.

Q *Should the follower of a religion have the right to try to convert people who belong to other faiths?*

Gender and sexuality

Many social issues are controversial and arouse strong feelings. Gender is one. Many women complain at the way they are represented in the western media. Tabloid (small-format, popular) newspapers show semi-nude photographs of models and film-stars, but rarely portray women as they really are. Some feminists have called for such photographs to be banned.

Q *Does a photograph which demeans women actively corrupt society, or should it just be seen as the product of a corrupted society? Is it dangerous – or just sad?*

In some countries and cultures it may be forbidden to portray women as the objects of men's desire, but instead they are often completely ignored by the media. In the Asian country of Afghanistan, for example, where women are required to remain heavily veiled, they are largely excluded from public life and their voice is silenced by the governing Islamic Taliban movement.

Attitudes towards sexuality in the media vary greatly from one country to another. In many countries same-sex relationships are illegal or taboo, and gay issues are censored. Even though homosexuality between adults is legal in Britain, a 1988 law made it illegal for schools to teach that a homosexual relationship was an acceptable basis for family life.

Languages and peoples

Language is another burning social issue in many parts of the world. There are at least 5,000, possibly as many as 10,000 different languages spoken in the world – but only 80 of these are official, government-approved languages.

The languages of minority peoples may be banned from the classroom and the law courts, or ignored by the broadcasting media. Some governments may ban the use of a language outright. Employers may refuse their employees the right to speak to each other in their own language. Censorship of minority languages is yet another way of maintaining government or majority control. Without a means of self-expression, a culture soon disappears.

> *We need a diversity of language because multilingualism is a normal and healthy part of the way human society is organised.*
>
> Dr David Dalby, director of Observatoire Linguistique, 1997

Many censorship issues revolve around questions of racism. Racism is the abuse of one ethnic group by another, normally arising from ignorance of other peoples' cultures or from the

In 1986, black children in Soweto, South Africa, protested against the use of the Afrikaans language in their schools. They wanted to be taught English. Fierce riots broke out against the racist government which then ruled the country.

mistaken belief that some sections of humanity are superior to others. Adolf Hitler, the leader of the German Nazi party in the 1930s, chose to blame all his country's problems on the Jews. Like the first Chinese emperor, he went in for burning books in public. Books written by Jewish authors were destroyed. Later, more than six million Jews were murdered.

Many people campaigning against racism today would in turn deny a public platform to anyone calling for policies like those of Hitler. Racist abuse has been made illegal in many countries.

German students made public bonfires of books by Jewish authors during the Nazi period of the 1930s. Books may be burned, but ideas are harder to destroy.

Q *Are laws the best way to combat racism?*

Q *Suppose that a book first published 100 years ago contains the racist language which was common in those days. Should it be removed from a modern edition of the book in order to avoid giving offence, or should it be left alone, as a piece of history?*

Artistic freedom

Censorship is very common in the world of the arts. In many countries, exhibitions of paintings or sculpture and concerts of music may be cancelled by the authorities.

Rappers rapped
In 1996 French rap stars Joey Starr and Kool Shen were found guilty of insulting the police in their songs. They were fined thousands of pounds, imprisoned for three months and faced a six-month ban.

Pop music has always been a victim of broadcast bans. When 'rock 'n' roll' appeared in the 1950s, it was banned on some US radio stations for being the 'devil's music' and too sexually explicit. In the 1960s, in the US and Europe, rock songs were banned for referring to drugs. In the 1970s punk groups were banned for using bad language. In the 1980s and 90s several rap singers in various countries were silenced for preaching violence and racism in their lyrics.

> *Any musical innovation is full of danger to the whole state and ought to be prohibited.*
>
> Plato, Greek philosopher (c427-347BC)

The arts may also be banned simply on the grounds of aesthetics – the idea of what is beautiful, of what the role of art should be, of 'good taste'. Abstract art, jazz and pop music have all been banned at times during the last 100 years.

This is La Maja Vestida by the Spanish artist Francisco de Goya y Lucientes (1746-1828). Goya originally showed the model naked, but his painting was banned by Kings Carlos III and IV – so he produced the clothed version shown below. Goya was an official painter to the Spanish court, and often ran into trouble with his liberal political views as well as his ideas about decency.

Sick art?

In September 1997 demonstrators in England called for the banning of an art exhibition at London's Royal Academy, because it included a portrait of convicted child murderess Myra Hindley. The artist, Marcus Harvey, had made up the picture from children's handprints. Protestors complained that this was 'sick' and would cause offence to the relatives of the children who had been killed. They defaced the painting. Supporters of the gallery said that it was legitimate for a painting to challenge, shock and provoke debate.

Can there any be any rules about what is good art and what is bad art?

Good or bad censorship?

Clearly, issues of censorship and information control run right through every strand of daily life. Could society survive if all censorship was removed? Could it survive if all channels of communication were vetted and controlled? Or does it depend on the motives in each case?

'Bad' motives for censorship might include a love of power and control for its own sake, the promotion of crime or injustice, the suppression of political or religious freedom, the desire of a company to create a trade monopoly. Good motives might include democracy and the public interest, the protection of life, the safeguarding of vulnerable or young people, the prevention of racial hatred.

Where is the dilemma? Isn't the question simply one of ethics, of what is right and wrong? Well, ethical questions are rarely simple. Nearly all censors claim to be acting in the public interest, but safeguarding the legitimate interests of one group may endanger the legitimate interests of another.

...if we deny freedom of speech to opinions we hate, we weaken the legitimacy of our entire political system.

Professor Ronald Dworkin, 1997

4. HOW DOES CENSORSHIP OPERATE?

Indirect censorship takes many forms around the world. For example, a theatre or art gallery may be closed if grants or sponsorship deals are withdrawn for political reasons. Universities may have government research funding removed or reduced, and any schools that do not toe the government line may find that they are given no money to buy books or equipment.

> *We must try to find ways to starve the terrorist and the hijacker of the oxygen of publicity on which they depend.*
>
> Margaret Thatcher,
> former British Prime Minister

> **Should the arts avoid sponsorship if this lays them open to censorship by the sponsor?**

> **Don't make waves – or else...**
> In the southeast Asian country of Indonesia, in 1997, the government appointed a new Minister of Information, called General Hartono. His attitude to information soon became clear when he issued a warning to journalists – if they wrote stories which caused trouble, the government would revoke their publishing licences.

In many countries teachers are registered as civil servants, which makes them directly accountable to the government. Any teachers with dissident views may find themselves sacked.

Journalists may be unwilling to cover a story if they think they will lose their job or their press card as a result.

Voluntary codes of control, where journalists are expected to avoid covering certain topics in the interests of 'responsible' journalism, are often referred to as 'self-censorship'. This form of control may help to curb the worst kind of sensational reporting, racist headlines or articles which intrude upon people's grief or privacy.

Journalists clearly have a duty to act responsibly and self-censorship must be preferable to violent or extreme censorship from outside. However, the pressures on a journalist are many and subtle, and self-censorship may serve the interests of those in power every bit as effectively. It is often much harder to spot. In some countries self-censorship has official status, so that the press or advertising industry is required to 'police' itself by setting up professional bodies that agree on certain standards and procedures and take action against colleagues who break them. For example, the body might order a newspaper to print an apology, or give someone the right of reply to a published article.

An editor may stop a report being published if it is critical of a firm that buys advertising space in his or her newspaper, or of a firm that has links with the newspaper's owner.

Q *Is a censored voice better than no voice at all? Should a newspaper editor go along with a certain amount of censorship if the alternative is total closure?*

Pressure to keep your mouth shut may be brought to bear in many ways. Public opinion is a powerful one. Might this be a sort of censorship by your neighbours? Your colleagues may refuse to speak to you. The public may stop buying goods in your shop. Your parents won't let you play with the children next door. No laws have been broken, but you feel intimidated and remain silent. It is not too difficult to imagine situations where this might occur – in industrial disputes, in local quarrels, in communities split by religious differences, racism or criminal activity.

Direct censorship

Direct censorship is more obvious. Its aim is to stop a medium functioning, to interfere with or close down channels of communication. In some countries, censorship of this sort takes place every day. In others, direct censorship is more limited, but may be expanded to cover more areas during wartime or national emergencies. In many countries photographers are forbidden to take pictures of operations by the security forces, of military bases or vehicles. Public meetings are made illegal. Mail is opened and censored or destroyed, telephones are tapped or disconnected, printing presses and newspapers are closed down, television programmes or film screenings may be banned. At political protests, cameras or film may be seized by police officers or soldiers. Direct censorship in the public eye is often intended as a deterrent, discouraging others from taking action.

Using the law

Rightly or wrongly, laws may be used to restrict communication. People who insult or defame someone else by word of mouth may be taken to court for slander. If the same material takes the form of the written word or a picture, people may be accused of libel. In principle, the idea is a fair one. In practice, the legal process is so expensive that it keeps many ordinary people silent and may put a magazine off

A newspaper rolls off the press. How might it be stopped? The press could be sabotaged or just turned off. It could be halted by legal order or on the word of the owner.

publishing facts even if it knows them to be true.

An injunction or legal order may be taken out to stop a television programme being shown or a newspaper being published until a legal challenge has been cleared by the courts. The intention of such laws is to ensure that the law responds rapidly to what may prove to be an injustice. However, they may also be used by lawyers as a way of gagging the media until the story is no longer topical.

Lashed for libel

In some countries the penalties for libel are not just financial. In 1997 two journalists from Yemen, named Abdul Jabbar Saad and Abdullah Saad, were convicted of libel. Their sentence was 80 lashes and a year's ban on writing.

Laws of copyright also place limits on free communication. They prevent writing, music or art being copied by someone else, or being published without permission. In this case the restriction of a medium actually protects the rights of an author or composer. Copyright is intended to protect writers, artists and publishers for up to 70 years after their death, but in practice it is hard to enforce the law internationally. Books, CDs, tapes and videos are all copied and distributed without permission. This is called 'pirating'.

Should textbooks be exempted from copyright in countries where schools are too poor to buy them?

The ultimate deterrent

In July 1997 the body of a man was found dead in the Ajolotero river, in Mexico. He was called Leonicio Pintor García and he had been a journalist on a newspaper called El Sol. García had been tortured, by persons unknown. He was just one more statistic in a world where many journalists who ask awkward questions suddenly 'disappear' and are never seen again. At the end of 1997 the International Federation of Journalists (IFJ) also recorded the killings of 46 other journalists and media workers around the world, and noted a further 15 incidents which were still being investigated.

Such tactics are a form of terrorism. Terrorism is not only carried out by small groups prepared to use violence to achieve their aims. It is carried out just as often by governments against their own people.

The Dirty War
In 1976 a 'dirty war' began in the South American country of Argentina. Military rulers seized power and banned all political parties. Anyone who spoke up in protest faced torture or murder by squads of thugs. In the following six years of this reign of terror, over 10,000 people just disappeared, and are believed to have been killed. Tens of thousands more were arrested, tortured and imprisoned without trial.

Assassination is the extreme form of censorship.
George Bernard Shaw, 1916

Twisting the message

Finally, censorship may operate in rather more complicated ways. For example, the flow of information may be distorted rather than cut off. Lies and smears may be used to discredit someone as a reliable source of information. Invented stories,

Photographs or film may show soldiers in heroic poses. The images may be completely genuine, or they may have been taken when the soldiers were not at risk. How can we know?

My definition of a free society is a society where it is safe to be unpopular.
Adlai Stevenson, US politican, 1952

Extreme, life-threatening censorship was repeated by dictators all over the world during the twentieth century, from Cambodia to Iraq. For political reasons, some of these brutal dictatorships were actually supported or funded by powerful democratic countries, who claimed to be champions of freedom.

either complete falsehoods or half-truths, may be put out as part of a propaganda campaign. These may prevent communication of the truth just as effectively as other methods of censorship.

> **The rulers... are the only ones... who may be allowed to lie for the good of the state.**
>
> *Plato, Greek philosopher (c427-347BC)*

Is it ever morally acceptable to publish a lie?

False stories may even be given credibility by faked photographs. In eastern Europe, during the 1950s and 60s, politicians who had fallen from favour (such as Czech statesman Alexander Dubček) were often removed from official photographs. The public never knew that these politicians had ever been present – they had been turned into non-persons.

Today, many newspapers use photographs whose images have been manipulated or altered by computers. This has become so common that it has been suggested that electronically altered images should be marked with a special symbol to warn the reader that these are not true photographs. In 1998 media trade unions in Germany reached an agreement with publishers that manipulated pictures would be clearly marked with an **M**.

Spot the difference! Computers have made it easier than ever to censor visual images in newspapers and on television.

5. SECRECY AND PRIVACY

In 1994 President Bill Clinton ordered the release of a number of classified (secret or restricted) documents held in the United States National Archives. They numbered 44 million. That left no less than 281 million archive documents still classified – and didn't even start on the top secret files held by the US military or by the secret service, the Central Intelligence Agency (CIA). In 1997 another long-standing secret was revealed – the year's budget for financing the CIA, namely 26 billion dollars.

Official secrets

Almost all countries spend large sums of money on secret activities and on hiding information from the public eye. Dictators and repressive governments may never open up their files. They are not accountable to the public. In some democratic countries, such as Australia, Canada and the United States, there are freedom of information laws which guarantee limited public access to certain data. The British government is in the process of preparing similar legislation to put before parliament.

In 1989 the Berlin Wall was knocked down. Originally raised by the communist government of East Germany, it had divided the city for 28 years. The East German state soon collapsed and Germany was reunited. East German citizens now broke into the headquarters of the State Security Police, and got a chance to see for themselves the thousands of secret files that had been held there.

Official secrets may include details of the everyday discussions of governments and committees, details of the armed forces and secret service organisation. In many countries these details are not released for 30 or even 50 years.

Official secrecy is defended by rulers because it is said to be 'in the national interest'. Governments do have a clear duty to protect the lives and well-being of the public and of government employees, such as soldiers, spies or diplomats. This obviously involves concealing any kind of information that might help terrorists or an enemy. For that reason, official secrecy is always increased greatly during wartime.

Q *Should the public receive more information or less information from their government during times of war?*

Cover-ups

The trouble is, official secrecy can also be used to conceal mistakes made by the governments and to deny the opposition access to embarrassing facts. It could be used for example to conceal a country's economic problems, either from its own people or from countries wanting to open up businesses there.

British naval officers censor sailors' letters home during the Second World War (1939-45). It is normal to censor mail in wartime, in case it gives away secrets of troop movements to enemy spies.

It could be used to hide corruption or criminal activities by government officials. It could be used to conceal information about pollution or risks to public health.

> *It is error alone that needs the support of government. Truth can stand by itself.*
>
> Thomas Jefferson,
> US statesman (1781)

Where there's smoke, there's no fire

Many countries have nuclear power stations and these are often state-owned. Details about how they operate are often kept secret, because they contain highly dangerous materials. However, this secrecy has in the past been used to cover up major nuclear accidents which threatened the lives of the public. It took successive British governments over 30 years to reveal the true seriousness of a fire at one English nuclear plant (Windscale, later renamed Sellafield) in 1957. In this case, was secrecy really 'in the public interest'?

This plant at Sellafield, in England, is designed for the reprocessing of highly dangerous radioactive materials. Is the public entitled to know the whole truth about sites which may affect their health or security?

Trade secrets

Some of the most secretive organisations in the world are industrial and commercial companies. They may wish to keep the recipe for a soft drink or the design for a new car or computer secret from the prying eyes of their rivals. They may wish to keep financial details away from companies who want to take them over. Many firms now have strict security on the doors, records of who checks in and out, identity badges for staff – all to keep out spies from other companies.

Trade secrets are also kept from the public. Does a product have a harmful affect on public health? Does a new drug have side effects? Are the full ingredients of a food product listed? Were the factory workers who produced the item properly paid? Has a mining, oil drilling or logging operation polluted the environment or destroyed the way of life of people in another land? Companies often try to avoid answering such embarrassing questions and may use more active, even extreme, types of censorship in order to stop the full truth coming out.

Did they hide tobacco truth?
*During the 1990s, many people with illnesses caused by smoking cigarettes took the tobacco companies to court in the United States and in other countries.
A key question kept coming up. When had the companies learned the truth about the links between smoking and disease? Did they keep their research secret and use advertising to encourage the public to keep on smoking this addictive drug?*

Companies may also keep all kinds of information secret from their own staff. This might concern working hazards or health and safety, the financial state of the company, how much other workers are paid or details of their rights to join a trade union.

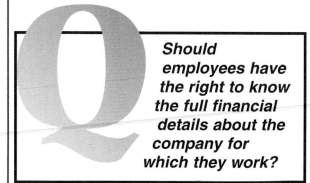

Should employees have the right to know the full financial details about the company for which they work?

Blowing the whistle

Secrecy in government or in industry may be strengthened by laws or by personal contracts which forbid a worker from revealing secrets, 'leaking' information or talking to the media. Sometimes, however, workers decide that it is actually in the public interest for them to break silence. If the government is trying to conceal a scandal, a civil servant or a secret agent might decide to tell the press – even if this breaks a binding legal agreement that they have signed. For example, a worker might alert the authorities if his company is asking him to tip poisonous waste illegally.

If you sign a job contract including a promise of secrecy, is it ever fair to break that agreement?

If you commit a foul during a game of football, the referee blows his whistle. In the same way, anyone who stands up and calls 'foul' in public life is called a 'whistle-blower'. Whistle-blowers risk losing their jobs and may face legal action or even violence. Mordechai Vanunu was an Israeli technician who told the *Sunday Times* newspaper in Britain that his country had developed a nuclear weapons arsenal. In October 1986 Vanunu was kidnapped by Israeli secret agents, smuggled back to Israel, given a secret trial and imprisoned. Some countries, such as Sweden, recognise that whistle-blowers can act in the public interest and have brought in laws to protect them from being victimised.

Private lives

Should everyone have a right to privacy? A section of the press, commonly known by the Italian term *paparazzi*, often hounds celebrities. Journalists and photographers peer into famous people's homes with telephoto lenses, raking through their rubbish bins, following them wherever they go and causing distress to their families. In 1997 a member of the British royal family, Princess Diana, was killed during a high speed car ride in Paris, France. There were suggestions that the car was being chased, as was often the case, by *paparazzi*.

In the old days men had the rack. Now they have the press.
Oscar Wilde, Irish writer (1856-1900)

Famous people often use publicity to make themselves wealthy and powerful and many enjoy appearing in the news. Is it realistic for them to then turn around and expect the press to leave them alone?

Filmstar Tom Cruise meets the press. Celebrities depend on the press, but may try to prevent it intruding upon their privacy.

What's in my file?

Many other censorship issues concern the conflict between individual privacy and the public's right to information. The rapid development of computer technology in the last 20 years has meant that a vast amount of information about individuals can now be stored electronically. This might include criminal records, medical records, political beliefs, details of how much people earn or even what they buy at the supermarket.

A European Convention on Data Protection was introduced in 1985, and since then many countries have used this agreement as a basis for data protection laws. These allow members of the public limited access to computer files or written records, so that they can make sure that the material held about them is up-to-date, relevant, correct, and secure from unauthorised access. Laws are also being considered in some countries to prevent the tapes from the security cameras, which survey city centres, being shown on public television without the permission of the people filmed.

Laws of privacy do exist, but they are of little use if they are abused in order to conceal corruption, incompetence or criminal activity. Journalists must be able to investigate freely without facing a smokescreen in the name of 'privacy'.

6. FREE SPEECH - A BASIC RIGHT?

Imagine you live in a country that allows very little freedom. You want to start up a band, but the government controls all the radio programmes and won't allow the kind of music you like to be performed. Perhaps you want to write political songs. Just by practising with your friends you risk attracting the attention of the secret police as a rebel. You have little choice. You either give up your music, or else you record tapes secretly and pass them on privately to people you can trust – even if this means you could be thrown in jail.

How personal is a personal stereo? Do you have a right to listen to any music you want to? Or should the content of pop songs be vetted by the government or by your parents? Should children have fewer rights than adults?

Similar ways of opening up channels of communication are often used by poets or writers. In the Soviet Union and neighbouring countries, during the 1960s and 70s, writers who could not be published officially would photocopy their work and secretly pass it around as a '*samizdat*' ('self-published') publication. Illegal, secret communication networks of this sort are often described as 'underground'. In the late 1980s, just before the communist governments of central and eastern Europe collapsed, there were about 50 *samizdat* periodicals circulating in Poland alone.

> **What one writer can make in the solitude of one room is something no power can easily destroy.**
>
> Salman Rushdie,
> author of The Satanic Verses

Human rights, human duties

Many people believe that open expression, or free speech, is an essential human right. By referring to free speech as a human right, we suggest that it is a basic need, without which human society couldn't survive.

> **Beneath the rule of men entirely great, the pen is mightier than the sword.**
>
> Edward Bulwer-Lytton,
> British novelist (1803-73)

The idea of natural human rights was championed by an English campaigner called Thomas Paine, whose book *The Rights of Man* was published in 1791-92. Paine supported revolutions in North America and France and his fiery ideas brought him into all sorts of trouble with the censors of his day. Most other writers in the 1700s believed that any notion of human rights was pure nonsense. Kings ruled the land with the blessing of God, they said, and free speech would only disrupt the natural order of things and disturb society.

Today the idea of natural human rights is much more widely accepted. But are rights absolute, do they apply in all situations? Most people would say that rights are conditional upon certain duties the individual owes to society. Thomas Paine had already suggested as much when he wrote in 1776 that 'those who expect to reap the blessing of freedom must... undergo the fatigue of supporting it'. By 'undergoing fatigue', Paine meant facing up to hard or difficult work. If we demand basic rights such as freedom of speech, we must also offer the same rights to others. We must respect the lives, cultures and viewpoints of other people.

In 1789 the French people rose up and demanded basic human rights. However, within a couple of years the revolutionary government was itself ruling by strict censorship and terror.

Clashes of interest

Society is made up of many different groups. If it was a cake, it could be cut up in many different ways – along the lines of wealth or poverty, types of work, town and country, political attitudes, ethnic grouping and culture, language or dialect, literacy, religion, age, gender, ability or disability. Each social group has different interests, but at the same time each one shares interests with some of the others.

The social groupings overlap and form very complicated patterns. This makes it very hard to protect one social group without treading on the toes of another group. The situation becomes even more difficult when one of the groups is absolutely opposed to another.

Q *Should a political party that opposes free speech be allowed to use the communications media to put across its views?*

The only way to cope with so much variety is a political and social system that allows the people to make as many decisions as possible for themselves. This is commonly called democracy, which simply means 'rule by the people'. Just how that should be defined is a matter of endless debate. The ancient Greeks, who invented the word, excluded women, slaves and foreign residents from the public assembly in Athens.

Democracies normally aim to allow the votes of the majority of the population to decide questions of policy. However, for democracy to be just, it also has to allow the voices of minorities to be heard and recognised – the smaller groups who will never make up a large enough part of the population to form a majority.

South African voters queue for the polls in 1994, during the country's first ever democratic election. Since 1948 the voice of black South Africans had been silenced by white minority governments, under a racist system called apartheid.

Young people's rights

Most of the world's independent nations belong to the United Nations (UN), an organisation founded in 1948. It aims to encourage world peace and cooperation. In November 1989 the UN published its Convention on the Rights of the Child. This document sets out guidelines for governments on how to treat young people under the age of 18. Questions of censorship and free expression are central to the Convention. Here are some crucial extracts. How do they compare with your own experience?

• The child shall have the right to **freedom of expression***; this right shall include freedom to seek, receive and impart information and ideas of all kinds, regardless of frontiers, either orally, in writing or in print, in the form of art, or through any other media of the child's choice.*

• The exercise of this right may be subject to certain **restrictions***, but these shall only be such as are provided for by law and are necessary (a) for respect of the rights or reputations of others; or (b) for the protection of national security or public order, or of public health or morals.*

• Parties shall respect the right of the child to **freedom of thought***, conscience and religion.*

• No child shall be subjected to arbitrary or unlawful interference with his or her **privacy***...*

• Parties recognise the important function performed by the mass media and shall ensure that the child has **access to information** *and material from a diversity of national and international sources...*

• In those States in which **ethnic, religious** *or* **linguistic minorities** *or persons of* **indigenous** *origin exist, a child belonging to such a minority... shall not be denied the right... to enjoy his or her culture, to profess and practise his or her own religion, or to use his or her own language.*

If freedom is crushed...

One old argument is that free speech is not a human right but a privilege. Rulers in many parts of the world, from Myanmar (Burma) to Nigeria, still claim today that allowing debate and dissent will only bring social disorder. In reality it is the denial of free speech that creates social disorder in the long term.

> *...the peculiar evil of silencing the expression of an opinion is, that it is robbing the human race.*
>
> John Stuart Mill,
> English philosopher, 1859

7. DRAWING THE LINE

Lots of censorship, no censorship at all – or censorship for what is commonly agreed to be the good of society? The last option is probably the one that most people would choose. However the choices are not always as simple as they are made out to be.

Values vary. Muslim women who wear veils believe that it frees them from men's sexual attentions. Critics claim that it restricts their freedom.

Untangling issues

Pornography demeans women and corrupts the public. Or does it? How can corruption be measured? Can any links be proved between buying pornographic magazines and immoral behaviour? Does the definition of what is pornographic depend on facts or on values?

> **We see all pornography as violence against women.**
>
> Annie Blue, Women Against Violence Against Women, 1988

Cyberspace censorship

In May 1998, the press reported a landmark legal decision in Germany regarding internet censorship when the manager of a service provider, CompuServe Germany, was convicted because some of the many thousand users of the service had called up child pornography images. Both defence and prosecution had decided that he could not be held responsible, but the judge still found him guilty. He was given a two-year suspended sentence.

Should a religion or cult which encourages young people to leave their families be allowed to spread its message?

Many religious people would simply say that pornography is a sin, forbidden in their scriptures and offensive to God. Other people would say that pornography is wrong because it encourages social evils, such as the abuse of women. Others claim that pornography is a harmless fantasy, an escape valve which reduces the pressure on individuals and probably prevents social evils actually taking place. Pornography has certainly existed since early times, and all the attempts to censor it since the days of ancient Rome have failed.

> *I am not trying to claim 'porn' as a worthwhile artistic genre. Pornography is obscene, debasing and disgraceful. The trouble is, so am I. I'm sorry...*
>
> Comedian David Baddiel, 1994

Another problem that would have been familiar to the ancient Romans is that of violence as entertainment. The Romans used to come in vast crowds to watch people fighting each other to the death or being torn apart by wild animals. In the last 20 years there has been a great increase in the violence shown on television, film and videos.

The Roman crowds loved to watch gladiators being killed in the arena. Today's video violence may be acted out rather than real, but it is still sickening. Is the fight for censorship on moral grounds a losing battle against human nature?

Q *If everyday life is violent and people often use obscene language, doesn't an artist have a duty to show society as it really is?*

Many people are worried that this media violence is affecting individuals and corrupting children. Mass killings by lone gunmen and murders by children seem to back up this view. The press has often been quick to point out links between particular videos and individual acts of terror. These links are actually very hard to prove. For example, children often boast they have seen violent videos that they haven't. It is also said that children don't associate screen violence with the real thing. They realise it is pure fantasy.

Many people disagree. They say that the media are already known to exert great power. If we are influenced by advertising, then we are also bound to be influenced by images of violence on the screen. Could it be that screen violence only affects a small number of people who are already mentally disturbed? If so, should everyone be restricted because of the danger posed by a few? How would it be possible to decide who should be allowed to see violent films and who shouldn't?

Video violence at fault?
In April 1996 a lone man, Michael Bryant, for no apparent reason, savagely gunned down twenty tourists visiting the historical prison settlement of Port Arthur, in Tasmania. As in similar cases elsewhere in the world, many people wondered if the massacre had been inspired by violent, gun-toting heroes and villains on film or video. As a result, the Federation of Australian Commercial Television Stations decided to review its code of conduct and to reconsider its censorship of films and videos.

> *There is no evidence that the portrayal of violence for good or 'legitimate' ends is likely to be less harmful to the individual, or to society, than the portrayal of violence for evil ends.*
>
> Independent Broadcasting Authority
> Guidelines on the portrayal of violence, UK

Common sense?
Other issues are perhaps clearer. Whether your judgement is formed by your religious beliefs or simply by the desire for a better society, it is clearly wrong to publish lies about someone or to preach hatred for your fellow human beings.

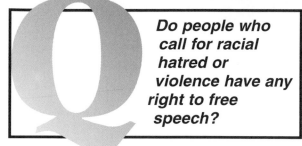

Q *Do people who call for racial hatred or violence have any right to free speech?*

Isn't censorship largely a question of common sense? Perhaps so, but common to whom? Many censorship decisions are based on prejudice rather than fact. Many public inquiries have been set up to try to evaluate the actual effect of, for example, violence and pornography. All provide interesting arguments, but few draw any firm conclusions. Those that do are often immediately countered and challenged by another report. The public remains confused.

Who decides?

If a line has to be drawn between what is permitted and what isn't, who should draw it? Should it be the government, or people appointed by the government? Should all censorship issues be covered by clear laws which are voted in or out by the public?

Q *If a newspaper is offensive, who is to blame – the journalists who produce it or the public who buy it?*

Who decides upon social controls such as censorship? Is it up to a democratic assembly or parliament, such as the German Bundestag? And if the assembly decides in principle, who should consider each individual case?

Should the decisions be left to psychologists or sociologists, as people who understand how images and words affect people? Should it be left to religious leaders? Or should censorship be left in the hands of the media operators, the broadcasters and publishers?

It might be argued that by calling for other people to censor material, we are avoiding our responsibility as individuals. Do we need protecting? Surely it is our ability to make moral judgements that defines our humanity.

Q

Is the off-switch the only truly moral censor?

Shouldn't each and every one of us decide for ourselves what to watch on television, which plays to see, which

Images pour into a newsroom from all over the world. Deciding which images to use or not may have to be a snap decision.

books to read? In reading this book you are examining moral dilemmas and drawing your own conclusions. You would not like to be told what those conclusions ought to be.

> *Since... the knowledge and survey of vice is in this world so necessary to the constituting of human virtue, and the scanning of error to the confirmation of truth, how can we more safely and with less danger scout into the regions of sin and falsity than by reading all manner of tractates and hearing all manner of reason.*
>
> John Milton, English writer, 1644

Reaching agreement

Censorship issues are complicated. They arouse strong and often contradictory feelings which can in themselves cause social unrest. As with many social issues, there may not be any clear-cut or easy answers. Any policy agreed must be realistic and workable, taking into account the medium in question and the social problems actually created, rather than imaginary ones.

It is possible to argue whether the same principles should apply to everyone in the world equally, or whether they should be relative to a particular culture. In the real world, censorship laws do reflect the culture which frames them. In a country in which 90 per cent of the population is Muslim, for example, censorship laws are bound to tie in with Islamic beliefs. The important point is that the censors are democratically accountable, that their rulings are essentially just – and that dissent is permitted.

8. REGULATION AND CONTROL

How is censorship delivered? Let's take a closer look at some of the mechanisms which are put in place to regulate and control the media.

Q | **Could a society exist without any censorship controls at all?**

Legal frameworks

The US Constitution or Bill of Rights is a document which sets out the legal principles upon which the country is to be governed, and its First Amendment is a clear statement that censorship will be held in check. In 1996 the First Amendment was used to overturn a new law which had been designed to protect young people from coming across obscene material on the internet, the Communications Decency Act. Many democratic countries have bills of rights or constitutions which offer limited guarantees of free speech. Of course these do not mean that censorship doesn't take place in these countries.

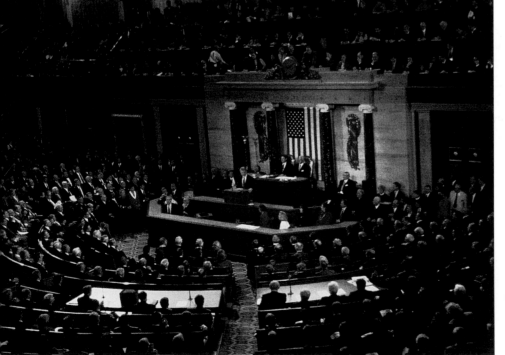

A legal constitution, such as that of the United States, is a useful mechanism for defining and guaranteeing human rights.

Free to criticise?

In 1998, US television 'chat show' hostess Oprah Winfrey was taken to court in Amarillo, Texas. During one of her shows, a vegetarian had criticised modern methods of cattle raising and meat production, explaining how they had already resulted in dreadful diseases such as BSE ('mad cow disease') breaking out in Great Britain. In response, Oprah had shuddered and wondered out loud if she could ever eat another hamburger. Texas cattle producers claimed that her comments affected the market in beef 'futures' and that she was defaming their product on television. Oprah's defence was based upon the 'First Amendment' to the US Constitution, which guarantees freedom of speech to all American citizens. This was upheld by the court. The cattle producers had to prove instead that Oprah Winfrey's comments were a malicious attempt to damage their trade. They lost their case.

Congress shall make no law respecting an establishment of religion, or prohibiting the free exercise thereof; of abridging the freedom of speech, or of the press; or the right of the people peaceably to assemble, and to petition the government for a redress of grievances.

First Amendment to the
United States Constitution

Judicial decrees may not change the heart, but they can restrain the heartless.

Martin Luther King,
US civil rights leader (1963)

Oprah Winfrey, top TV 'chat show' hostess, won her 1998 legal battle with the Texas cattle producers because, as a US citizen, she was entitled to freedom of speech. Big firms and other commercial interests often try to use the law to silence critics of their products.

By way of contrast, the constitution of the United Kingdom is simply the body of law as it has developed over many hundreds of years. Rights such as free speech are determined by the outcome of previous cases, or legal precedents. There is no overriding guarantee of individual rights. As the law stands in England and Wales, there are some 50 laws which can be used to silence journalists.

Legal mechanisms for limiting free speech are backed up by penalties. People found guilty of breaking the law might be fined, or imprisoned. Offending items might be confiscated. For example, during one series of raids in 1997, the Malaysian authorities seized 2,393 videos and compact discs that they declared to be pornographic. The 23 people they arrested faced fines or prison sentences. In some countries, such as China, legal penalties may be very severe.

Censorship boards

Many censorship decisions are carried out by official bodies or by committees of media representatives. Some of these are preventive, being set up by governments to vet communications media such as plays, films or videos before their release. Others are created in order to draw up practical guidelines for the media, or to consider complaints about newspaper articles, advertisements or broadcasts which have already appeared. The decisions of these bodies may be simply advisory or they may be legally binding.

Official censors face an almost impossible task as soon as they try to convert general moral principles into a detailed code of what is acceptable and what is not. Between 1934 and

Boards of censors have to decide which films are suitable for which age group. It is then up to the ticket office staff to decide whom they will let in to see the film.

1968, films produced in Hollywood, in the United States, had to be vetted before screening by the film industry's own censorship board, the Production Code Administration. Some of its decisions seem laughable to many Americans today. For example, a kiss on screen could only last for a maximum of 30 seconds. One second more and it had to be cut! Even married couples could not be shown on screen sharing a double bed.

> **Do you think young people are more at risk from the portrayal of sex or from the portrayal of violence on screen?**

Much of the discussion by censorship bodies today revolves around the question of whether the supposed violence or obscenity is gratuitous, or whether it serves an artistic purpose. The difficulty for the censors is that 'artistic value' has never been easily defined. Indeed, some would say that by its very nature it cannot be defined (see page 24). Decisions taken in these circumstances have to be subjective rather than objective.

Codes and warnings

Much of the work carried out by censorship boards today involves the grading of material in order to warn the public of its content. Films and videos are given a code which advises how suitable they are for children of various age groups. These warnings may be backed up by laws making it illegal to allow a child into a cinema showing a film in an older age group, or illegal to rent out a video to a child who isn't old enough.

Broadcasters, too, are often expected to issue a warning before showing any programme which contains violence, obscene language, swearing or sexually explicit scenes. Some broadcasters operate a 'watershed', a time (say 9 o'clock in the evening) after which young people are not expected to watch television. Of course this is not a very effective method of censorship. It relies on the cooperation of the young people or their parents.

There is an electronic alternative. It is possible to build a microchip into a television or video-cassette player which can be programmed to respond to a signal and automatically turn off a film graded as violent or obscene if a parent so wishes. This is known as a V-chip ('v' for violence).

Does regulation work?

If regulations and controls are to be an effective brake on the media, they must have the support of the public and they must be easily enforced. Even if the censorship is put into operation, that does not necessarily mean it will solve the social problem being addressed. If the aim of moral censorship is to change human nature, it has been remarkably unsuccessful over the ages.

When censorship backfires

Regulation can have the opposite effect to the one intended. In Portugal, television channels responded to demands for more moral programming on television by showing a warning symbol on the screen before any nude scenes occurred. The trouble was that whenever the symbol came up, it actually increased the numbers of viewers.

A compact disc or book which has been banned often sells many more copies than one that hasn't. Marketing managers who say that 'any publicity is good publicity' may have a point. Pop groups have even been known to rewrite songs so that they *will* be banned, knowing that this will earn them the reputation of being controversial and rebellious. They are themselves manipulating the media!

> *The punishing of wits enhances their authority and a forbidden writing is thought to be a certain spark of truth that flies up in the faces of them that seek to tread it out.*
>
> Francis Bacon, English writer, 1589

A newspaper which is published with a blank space on its front page, where the original article was to have appeared, may simply show up the censor as an opponent of free speech. It may have precisely the opposite effect to the one intended.

In the 1980s British prime minister Margaret Thatcher made it illegal for the media to broadcast the words of any member of a political party such as Sinn Fein, which supported terrorism in Northern Ireland. The broadcasting media got around this ban by hiring actors to speak the words for them. Thatcher's act of censorship failed to block off the channels of communication. Would it have been more effective to have allowed anyone to speak who wanted to, and to let the audiences decide for themselves the value of the terrorists' argument?

This is an election rally in San Sebastian, Spain, in 1996. A hooded man speaks for Herri Batasuna, political wing of ETA, a group that has used bombing and assassination to advance the cause of independence for the Basque country. Is democracy best encouraged by giving a voice to such people or by censoring their message?

Q **If supporters of terrorism are banned from the media, is this a democratic or an anti-democratic measure?**

The making of martyrs
Enforcing censorship laws may make heroes of the accused instead of shutting them up. In 1998, Swedish police allowed Neo-Nazis (racist groups basing themselves on the German Nazis of the 1930s) to march, making Nazi salutes and shouting the Nazi slogan 'Sieg Heil' ('hail victory'). They weren't arrested, even though these actions were illegal under Swedish law. Should the marchers have been arrested as a stand against racism? Or should they have been ignored?

9. WORKING FOR THE FUTURE

Battles over free speech are not just fought out between communicators and censors, law-makers and mainstream politicians. The debate is often driven by public activists and campaigning groups. These may be made up of writers, journalists, media-users, parents, followers of religions, civil liberties organisations and all sorts of other interest groups.

Campaigners and watchdogs

Many pro-censorship groups have been set up over the last 50 years, such as the American Federation for Decency, the US Parents' Music Resource Centre, founded by Tipper Gore, or the UK Viewers' and Listeners' Association, founded by Mary Whitehouse.

Pro-censorship groups often support traditional religious-based views of morality. They seek out examples of obscenity or blasphemy. Such groups may take legal action against television programmes, demand warning stickers on certain CDs, picket cinemas, campaign against sex education in schools

Amnesty International campaigners in the American state of Texas protest about an execution in 1998. Groups such as Amnesty campaign for justice around the world. They have saved the lives of many imprisoned journalists and prisoners of conscience.

or against information on abortion or AIDS being made available to young people.

Other pro-censorship campaigners do not necessarily come from the ranks of traditionalists. They include many (but not all) feminists, who demand, for instance, that pornography be banned from newsagents, or anti-racist campaigners who want libraries to remove from their shelves children's books which they consider to be offensive. The critics of such groups sometimes describe them as 'politically correct', a sarcastic term which they really use to mean 'over-zealous' or 'interfering'. To others, however, such concerns reflect the only acceptable face of censorship, working to make the world a fairer place.

A large number of voluntary groups campaign against censorship. Some of them protest against all forms of censorship. These include some libertarian and anarchist groups. Anarchists are people who call for the abolition of all state controls and power structures. Their common political view is that society can be made to work by a series of voluntary agreements between individuals, and that all should be free to express themselves in whatever way they wish. Most other political philosophies approve of

censorship in some form or another.

Many more anti-censorship organisations concentrate on extreme political censorship, in the form of imprisonment and murder. This repression is often successfully targeted by groups such as Amnesty International and PEN (the International Association of Poets, Playwrights, Essayists and Novelists). These groups highlight the plight of people who have been silenced and of prisoners of conscience (people imprisoned for their beliefs) all over the world.

> *A journalist shall at all times defend the principle of the freedom of the Press and other media in relation to the collection of information and the expression of comment and criticism. He/she shall strive to eliminate distortion, news suppression and censorship.*
>
> from National Union of Journalists:
> Code of Conduct (UK and Ireland)

Various other 'watchdog' groups monitor all kinds of censorship in the world media. They turn the spotlight on to offending governments and corporations. These groups include journalists' trades unions, campaigns for press and broadcasting freedom, and publishers who air free speech issues. Many campaigners approach the problems of censorship as part of a general concern for civil liberties and open government.

Article 19, based in London, England, takes its name from the section of the United Nations' Universal Declaration of Human Rights which deals with freedom of speech. Reporters Sans Frontières, based in Paris, France, campaigns for the rights of journalists around the world. In the United States are the New York-based Committee to Protect Journalists and the Washington DC-based Freedom Forum. The latter runs the Newseum, a museum of the media opened in 1997, which includes a glass memorial to 1,000 journalists killed around the world between 1812 and 1996. Index on Censorship, based in London, publishes a wide range of articles about international censorship and free expression.

How can we find out about censorship problems in countries where the media are strictly censored?

What can be done?

Charters of human rights, such as those drawn up by the United Nations or the European Union are useful guidelines, but they need to be backed up by effective laws or else they are of little value.

And the news keeps on coming... headlines are flashed up at the Newseum, a US museum of the media. The debate over media censorship will not go away in the future. Indeed, new technologies will probably make it keener than ever.

Q *Why should we worry about censorship in some faraway country we know little about? What business is it of ours?*

Dictators are powerful and speaking up against them can be dangerous. Democratic governments and industries can be very powerful too and can easily brush aside individual complaints. The only way to campaign on issues such as free speech is to join up with other people and, where possible, to campaign – locally, nationally and internationally. International pressure by groups such as Amnesty International has been effective in reaching repressive rulers.

The poet John Donne, who lived 400 years ago, wrote that 'No man is an island'. He meant that our affairs are all interwoven, that we cannot stand apart from society and the world around us. This is truer than ever today. Communications media make the world seem smaller and smaller, and the same powerful corporations may control media in many different countries. Censorship affects the citizens of every country in the world and it therefore affects us too. If an artist is imprisoned, if a printing press is shut down or if a writer is beaten up and left for dead in some dark alley, it is our problem too. John Donne went on to write: 'Any man's death diminishes me, because I am involved in Mankind.'

Over to you

The debate about censorship has no simple answers. Censorship can be a positive benefit to society, preventing the strong from abusing the weak. It may yet prove to be a useful weapon in making the society we live in less violent. On the other hand censorship has always been used to protect the powerful against the common people, as an obstacle to democracy.

The censorship debate offers a series of perplexing dilemmas. Even if these cannot be solved, they cannot be ignored or avoided. Work out just how censorship affects you and the people around you. Whether you support a form of censorship or oppose it, discuss the issues with your friends, classmates or family. Listen to other people's views and concerns. Decide where you would like to draw the line. If you are free to speak, then speak - before somebody stops you.

GLOSSARY

accreditation the providing of an official permit or licence.

aesthetics the study of what is beautiful.

blacklist to make a list of prohibited people or items.

blasphemy an insult to God, offending holy scriptures.

censor (1) an official in ancient Rome, whose job was to check up on citizens (2) somebody who limits or prevents free communication.

censorship the limiting or prevention of free communication.

communist favouring a system of government in which some or all property is owned by the community or state, and in which the economy as a whole is directed by the state.

constitution the principles on which a country is governed.

copyright a law which prevents the copying of material without the author's or publisher's permission.

data *(singular: datum)* pieces of information, records.

democracy any system of government in which decisions are made by the people or by their elected representatives.

dictatorship a country ruled by a dictator, someone who has not been elected by the people.

editor (1) someone who checks and amends text before publication (2) the manager in charge of a newspaper or magazine.

e-mail a message sent directly from one computer to another using telephone links.

ethics a system of moral principles.

ethnic group a group of people sharing a common descent, language or way of life.

feminist supporting social, economic, political or personal policies which benefit women.

immoral offending against widely held views of what is right and proper.

injunction a legal order preventing somebody from doing something.

internet an international network of communication by computer.

interrogator someone who questions a prisoner.

judicial carrying out the law.

legitimate just, fair or permitted by law.

libel to damage someone's reputation with visual images or with the written word.

monopoly total control of a market, having no competition.

moral conforming with widely held ideas of what is right or proper.

motive the reason for doing something.

neutral not taking sides.

obscene indecent, offending widely held views about taste or morals.

official language a language authorised for public use by a government.

official secret a state secret, information withheld from the public.

partisan taking sides, biased.

pornography books, magazines, films, videos or other images intended to make people sexually excited.

propaganda (1) any information put out either in support of a particular cause or against it (2) false or misleading information put out for similar reasons.

publisher a person or firm who brings the printed word or music to the public, often in the form of a book, magazine or newspaper.

racism the belief that humanity is divided up into groups called 'races' and that some of these are inferior to others.

slander the crime of saying bad things about someone, of harming their reputation.

tabloid of newspapers, small-format, popular. Large-format, more up-market papers are called 'broadsheets'.

website an information point on the internet.

whistle-blower somebody who draws attention to wrong-doing in the organisation for which they work.

INDEX